March of the

C.O.W.S.

Creatures Of Wonderful Simplicity

ISBN-13:978-1534756762
ISBN-10:1534756760

DIONNE EDISON

………March of the C.O.W.S.

Creatures Of Wonderful Simplicity

Copyright © 2016 Dionne Edison

………**March of the C.O.W.S.**

Pam Ryans, Publishing Liaison
www.pamryans.com

ISBN-13:978-1534756762
ISBN-10:1534756760

Printed and Manufactured in the United States of America

FIRST PRINTING: August, 2016

DIONNE EDISON

DEDICATION

For people who enjoy the simple things in life.

CONTENTS

About These Poems

When I was a little girl my mother read to me daily. Her voice made words come alive in my mind and was music to my ears. That began my love for poetry. In kindergarten, I learned that Cows were loving mothers to their calves. When I came home and called my mother a cow it was not funny to her until she got the explanation. That began my fascination with cows. Times were simpler then.

This book honors my mother combining my love for poetry and fascination with cows. The cow pictures were photographed while driving the roads of west Alabama. 'Pretty Love' is the recurring conversation I had with my mother from my childhood until she died April 1993.

COWS

Cows are creatures of wonderful simplicity

Spending each day in blissful monotony

They eat grass or hay

No nerves to fray

They live life fully in slow velocity.

How does a black cow eat green grass and produce white milk?

Digestion!

The March of the Cows

Someone spread the word that the grass was greener on the other side.

The cows got the word and decided go see for themselves.

It wasn't long before the march was on and across the road they started.

Looking this way and that across the road they went;

Stopping traffic as they marched to greener pastures.

They decided that the grass was alright but realized that now the grass was really greener on the other side.

AT HOME

Chillin'

Relaxing on the

Green grass around the pond is

Cozy and comfortable.

Cow Jokes

Two horses, Sable and her friend Caramel were grazing in the field one day. As they are looking out over the field at the herd of cattle, Sable asked Caramel, "What did the Cow say to the Bull?" "I don't know, what?" asked Caramel. "Moooo over."

"Aw that was corny" said Caramel, laughing anyway.

"Think so?" said Sable.

Yea, I've got one for you. "What did the Bull say to the Cow?" asked Caramel. "What?" asked Sable. "You moooo over. I was here first!"

"Well, I guess this field is full of corn today," said Sable. Caramel and Sable continued to laugh and tell corny cow jokes all day.

Pretty Love

Sweetie, what are you doing?

    Looking at you Momma?

Why?

    I like looking at you?

Why?

    I think you are pretty?

Is that all?

    No.

What then?

I love you, Momma.

I love you, too, Sweetie.

It's Good

Down by the river side

A mid-day drink with friends is as

Good as good can be.

DIONNE EDISON

COWS

Creatures Of Wonderful Simplicity

Poem Definitions

An **Acrostic** is a poem, word puzzle or other composition in which certain letters form a word or words.

A **Limerick** consists of five lines. A limerick should have a rhyme pattern of aabba: This means lines 1, 2 and 5 rhyme and lines 3 and 4 rhyme. Also, lines 1, 2 and 5 generally have 7 – 10 syllables and lines 3 and 4 generally have 5 – 7 syllables.

A **joke** is something said or done that causes laughter and not to be taken seriously.

A **Free Verse** is poetry written with rhymed or unrhymed verse that has no set meter to it.

A **Haiku** is a Japanese poem. It consists of 3 lines and 17 syllables.

Each line has a set number of syllables: **Line 1** – 5 syllables **Line 2** – 7 syllables **Line 3** – 5 syllables

ABOUT THE AUTHOR

Dionne Edison, known as "Granny",
loves to write with and for her grands and other children.

Her words take you back to the innocence of childhood.

Remember "when" with her.

Contact Dionne at grannylusvyou@gmail.com
and share your moments of childhood innocence.